d south of
1878

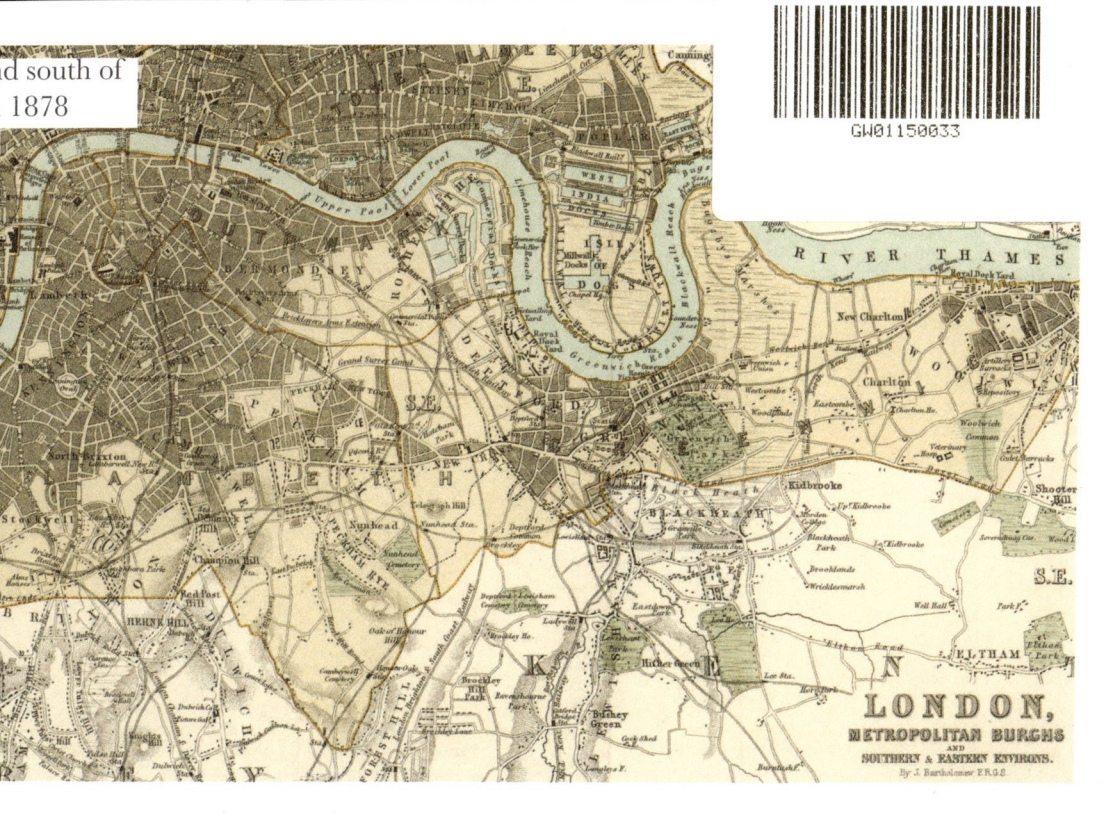

LONDON,
METROPOLITAN BURGHS
AND
SOUTHERN & EASTERN ENVIRONS.
By J. Bartholomew F.R.G.S.

LONDON

A LITTLE SOUVENIR

Chris Andrews Publications Ltd

Admiralty Arch

LONDON

Introduction

London is the capital and largest urban area of England and the United Kingdom. At its core, the ancient City of London, to which the name historically belongs, still retains its limited mediaeval boundaries; but since at least the 19th century the name "London" has also referred to the whole metropolis which has developed around it.

'Londinium' was founded by the Romans at a convenient crossing of the Thames, Tacitus describes a flourishing trading city existing in AD 67. The area was marshy but there was a low hill, roughly where the Bank of England now stands and it was here that the Romans chose to build a typical Roman city, primarily for military reasons. Their forum was where Leadenhall market now stands

When Anglo-Saxon settlers first moved into Britain in the 450s the importance of London was recognised and the city was often taken under direct control of the Essex overlords. Around 600 the first St. Paul's Cathedral was built within the Ludgate, supposedly replacing a pagan Saxon temple. The Vikings arrived in England in

The Tower of London and the skyline   5

6 Buckingham Palace and The Guards Band

numbers from the 830's and spent the winter of 871-2 in London, presumably within the walls. By 878 King Alfred the Great had become King of all the English and forced the Viking leaders to sue for peace. Through the 920s, the city became the most important commercial centre in England. In 1042, Canute's step-son, King Edward the Confessor of the old Saxon line, was invited to take up the throne of England. Perhaps best known for re-founding the great Abbey at Westminster, along with the adjoining palace, Edward died only a few weeks after construction work was completed in 1066.

After his victory at the Battle of Hastings, William the Conqueror's army ravaged much of the country in order to beat the English into submission. Though he burnt Southwark, he strategically avoided London and waited for the city's officials to recognise him as King. The Londoners

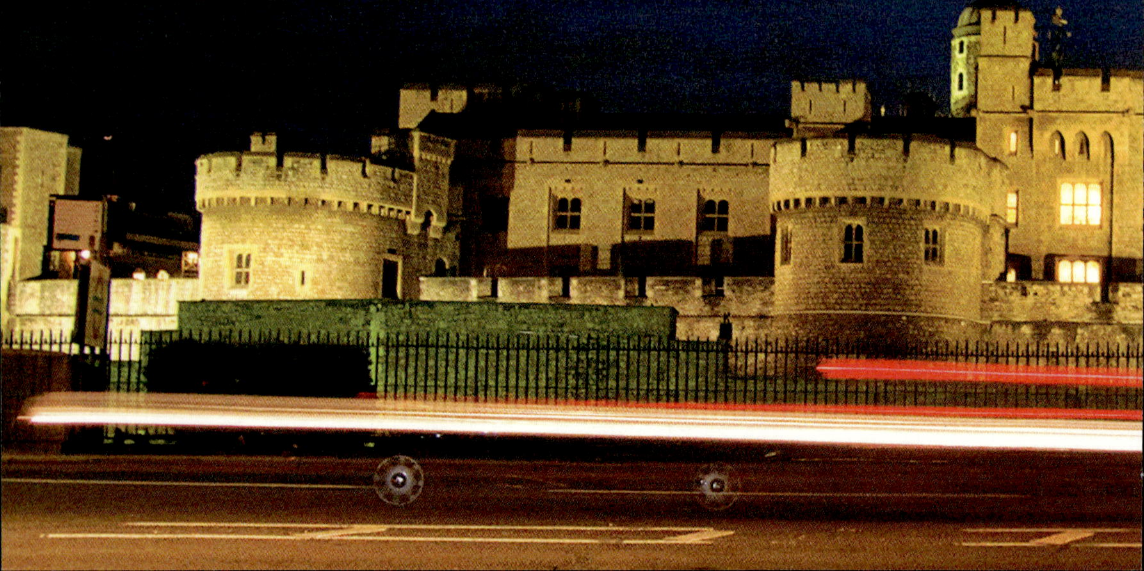

The Tower of London

quickly acquiesced and their swift action led the new monarch to grant their city the first formal charter of his reign.

London continued to ebbe and flow in her fortunes over the ages, the Plague in 1665 and the fire in 1666 shook London, but redevelopment around the 17th Century saw buildings like The Bank of England and most of the Bridges across the Thames, though Tower Bridge wasn't opened until 1894. The Victorians supervised the transformation of London into a modern city, installing sewers and underground railways (1863) beneath the ground of the capital, while overground railways in the 1830's and omnibuses (1850's) opened up the city, and the port of London experienced much of its final development.

HMS Belfast from Tower Bridge

Tower Bridge

12 Tower Bridge - mistaken for London Bridge by an American millionnaire, who transplanted the old London Bridge to Arizona, only finding out on delivery he hadn't bought Tower Bridge!

Modern day London is much influenced by commerce, especially banking and finance, though extensive rebuilding followed the two World Wars, there is plenty of historical importance still to see. London is one of the world's leading business, financial, and cultural centres, and its influence in politics, education, entertainment, media, fashion and the arts all contribute to its status as a major global city.

London boasts three World Heritage Sites: the Tower of London, the Palace of Westminster, (Houses of Parliament) and the historic settlement of Greenwich. It is a city that can be enjoyed by all and this little book shows some if its charm.

The Houses of Parliament or Palace of Westminster Greenwich

14 The Millennium Bridge and the Tate Modern

The Millennium Bridge is a feat of engineering, a suspension bridge held up by nothing but a set of steel cables

16 St Paul's Cathedral, designed by Sir Christopher Wren and built between 1675 and 1710 after its predecessor was destroyed in the Great Fire of London.

St Paul's west front

18   St Paul's Cathedral - details

St Paul's Cathedral

The West End - 'Theatre Land'

Theatre lights 21

22 Piccadilly Circus

Shakespeare's Globe Theatre on The South Bank 23

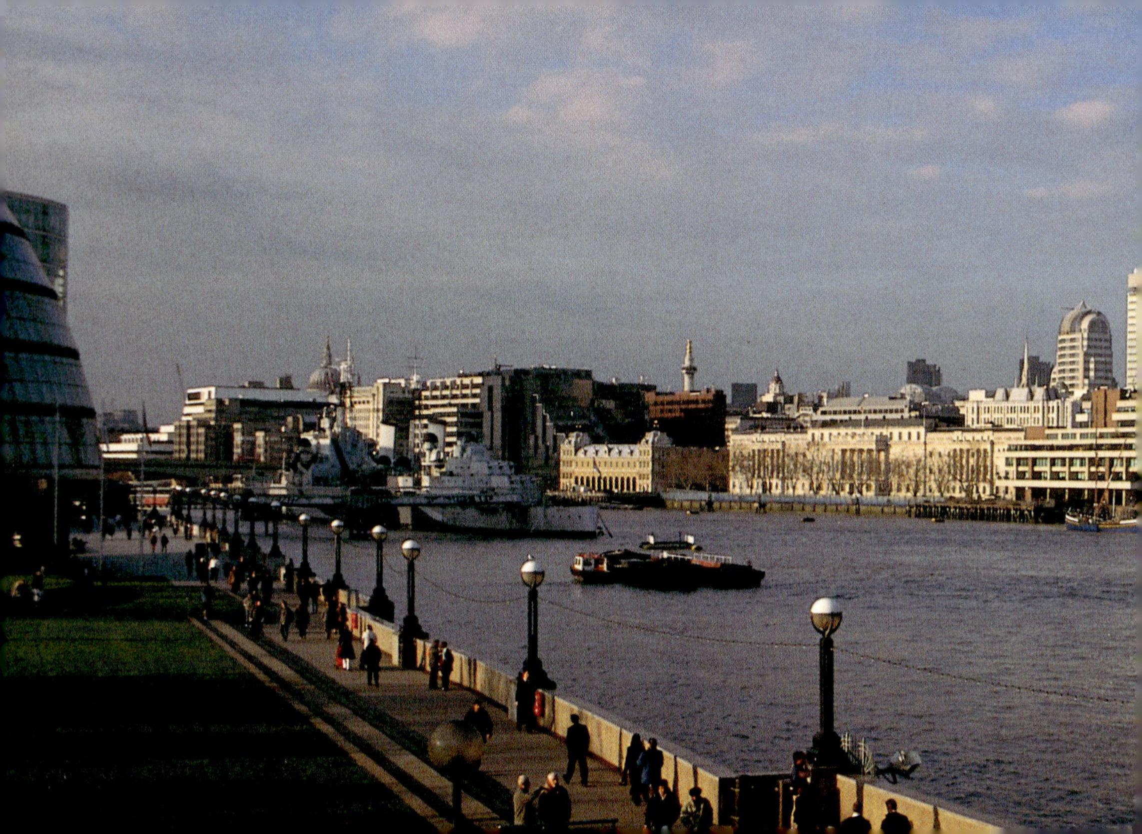

The Thames and The City

26 Embankment and The Houses of Parliament

Entertainments and shopping - at Covent Garden and Burlington Arcade   27

28 Covent Garden

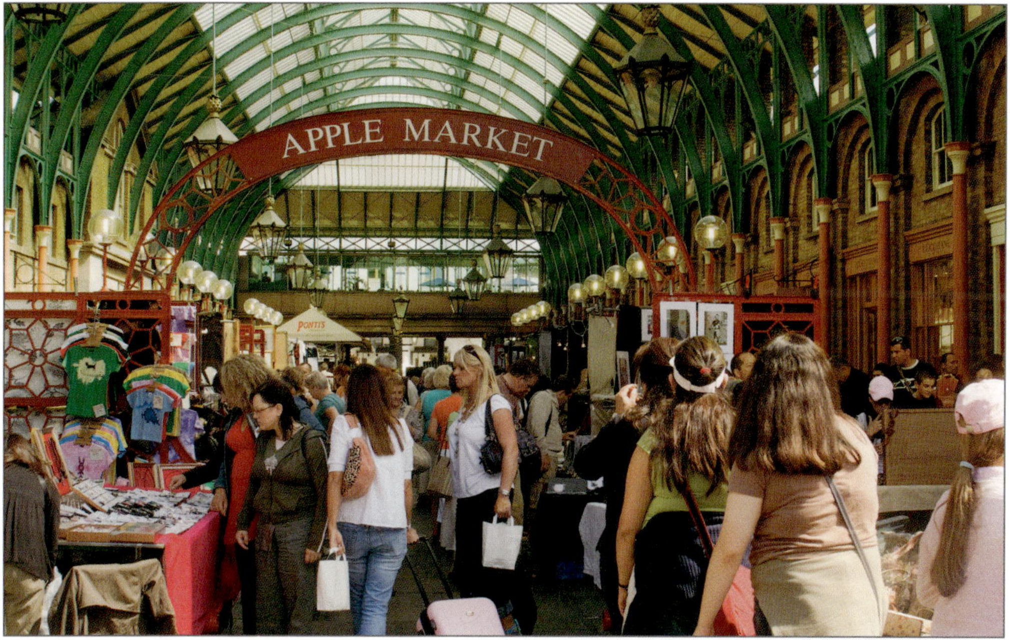
APPLE MARKET

30   Shop London! Hamleys world famous toy shop and the Selfridges statue

Harrods, Knightsbridge 31

32   China Town and Liberty

Underground Sign and the London Dungeon

34 London Signs

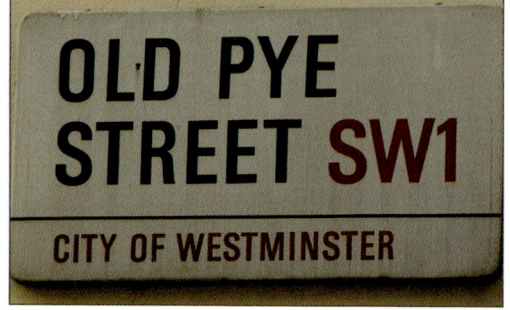

London Signs   35

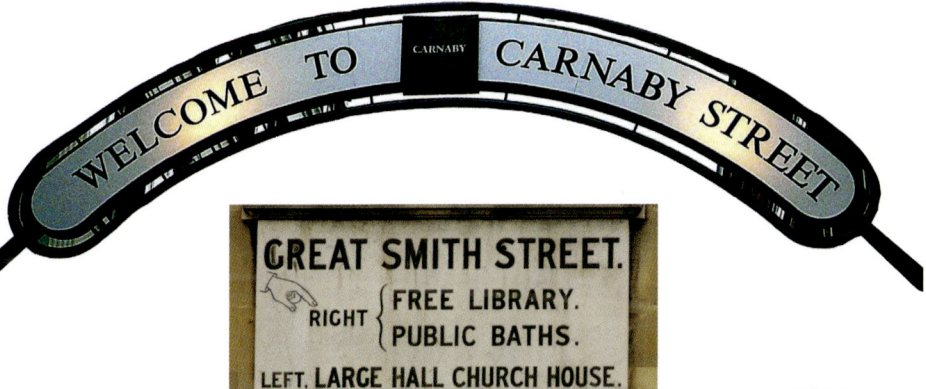

36 Fountain and Lion in Trafalgar Square

The National Gallery   37

38 Nelson's Column was built between 1840 and 1843 to commemorate Admiral Horatio Nelson's death at the Battle of Trafalgar in 1805

Trafalgar Square at dusk

THE EVENING STANDARD FOR 15p
OVER LONDON
Find out how at
eroscard.co.uk
Evening Standard

Fountain in Trafalgar Square

42 The Albert Memorial and The Royal Albert Hall from Kensington Gardens

Bridge over The Serpentine between Hyde Park and Kensington Gardens 43

44 St. James's Park is a 58 acre park in Westminster, the oldest of the Royal Parks of London

St James's Park

Guards Band at Buckingham Palace

46 Buckingham Palace from St James's Park

The Royal Horse Artillery in The Mall 47

48 Buckingham Palace, the official London residence of Her Majesty The Queen

Guards Band at Buckingham Palace   49

50 The statue of Queen Victoria and a detail from the Palace gates

The Houses of Parliament and The Thames

52 Big Ben, Westminster Bridge (with London bus) and The London Eye

The Palace of Westminster, also known as the Houses of Parliament, is where the two Houses of the Parliament of the United Kingdom meet.

54 Stonework on the Houses of Parliament

Houses of Parliament and Westminster Bridge   55

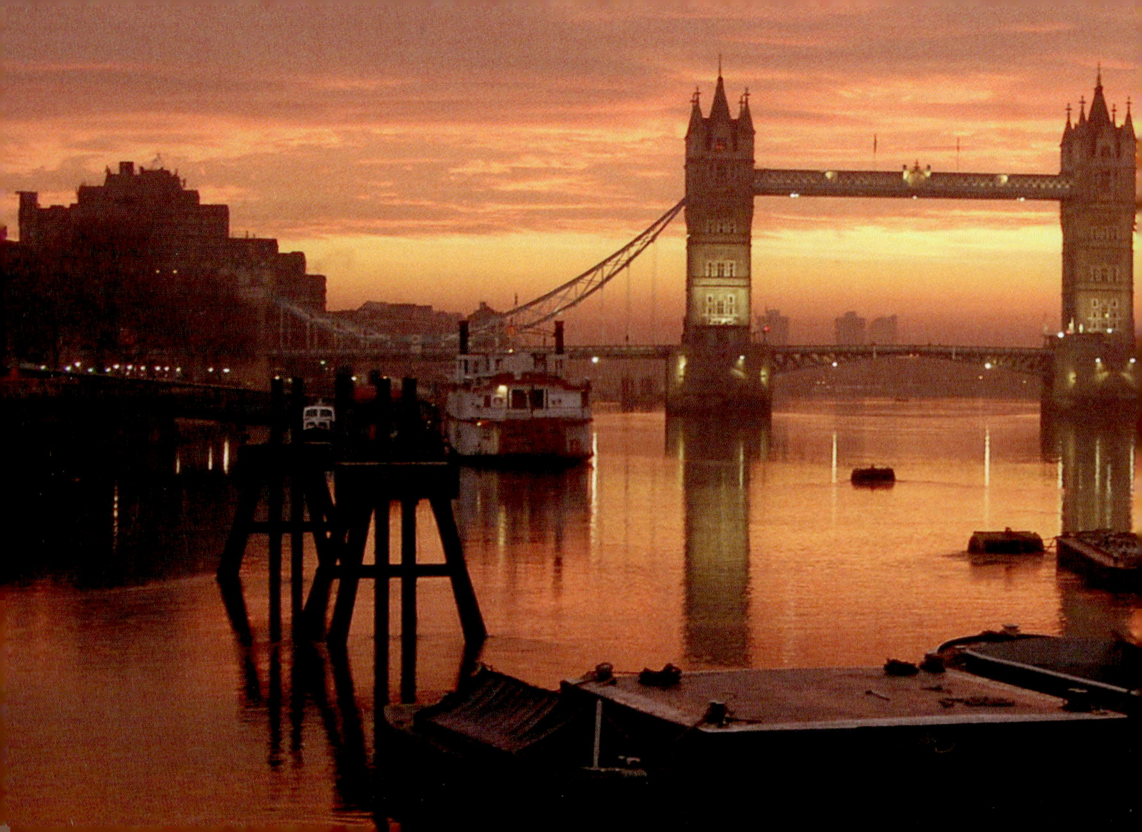

The Thames and Tower Bridge

58 The Royal Albert Hall, opened by Queen Victoria in 1871

Westminster Abbey, according to tradition the Abbey was first founded in 616

60 The Diana, Princess of Wales Memorial Fountain was started in September 2003 and officially opened on 6 July 2004 by Queen Elizabeth II

Kensington Palace a royal residence set in Kensington Gardens. Until 1997 this was the official residence of Diana, Princess of Wales

62   An original London Bus and The Cutty Sark

The Millennium Dome (The O2) and The Thames Barrier 63

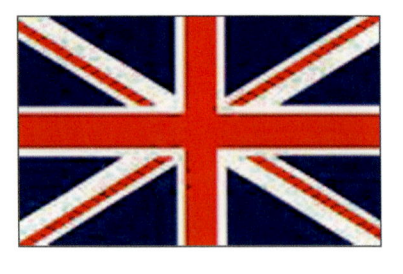

ISBN 978-1-905385-97-3

First published 2009 by Chris Andrews Publications Ltd, 15 Curtis Yard, North Hinksey Lane, Oxford. OX2 0LX
Telephone: +44(0)1865 723404 **www.cap-ox.com** © Chris Andrews Publications Ltd

Principle Photos: Carole and Reesy Andrews.

Additional material from Chris Andrews, Colin Nutt, Gareth Jones, Dan Mc Curry, Alamy and 'Morguefile.com' Thanks to Simon Crutchley for permission to quote from Londontourist.org
All rights reserved. No part of this publication may be reproduced, stored in a retrieval system, or transmitted, in any form or by any means, without prior permission of the copyright holder. The right of Carole, Reesy and Chris Andrews as authors of this work has been asserted by them in accordance with the Copyright, Designs and Patents Act 1988.

Front Cover: Buckingham Palace   Title page: Admiralty Arch   Back cover: Harrods and The Union Flag

Chris Andrews

Chris Andrews work is known throughout England and the Channel Islands, and is seen in a variety of publications including calendars, posters, fine art prints and books.

This 'Little Souvenir' series attempts to show something of the unique charm of London in an attractive and portable form and features the work particularly of Carole and Reesy Andrews For information on all our publications see

**Chris Andrews
Publications Ltd
www.cap-ox.co.uk**